P9-DUU-796

Pig Pig Grows Up
by David McPhail

SCHOLASTIC INC.
New York Toronto London Auckland Sydney

ISBN 0-590-40416-4

12 11 10 9 8 7 6 5 4 3 2 1   6 7 8 9/8 0/9

Printed in the U.S.A.   09

Pig Pig was the baby of the family. His brothers and sisters had grown up and left home long ago. But Pig Pig refused to grow up.

He still wore his sleep suit, though it was much too tight, and he continued to sleep in his crib, even though his feet hung over the end.

At breakfast, Pig Pig sat in his high chair.
He ate Pablum and strained fruit.

When his mother had marketing to do, Pig Pig
insisted on being pushed in the stroller.

And at the market, Pig Pig would squeal and cry
loudly until his mother bought him whatever it
was that he wanted.

If his mother suggested that he fix his own
supper because she was just too tired, Pig Pig
would pout and say, "I can't! I'm only a baby!"

Pig Pig's mother grew tired of it.

"You're a big pig now, Pig Pig," she said.

"You've got to grow up."

But when she took away his old blanket and
bought him a *real* bed, he sobbed like a baby
all night long.

And when Pig Pig's mother packed away all
of his baby clothes and gave him grown-up
clothes, Pig Pig cried and cried.

"I want my baby clothes," he screamed. "I'm
only a baby!"

So Pig Pig's mother gave in again, and nothing
more was ever said about Pig Pig's growing up—
until one day, on the way home from the market.

Pig Pig's mother had a very hard time pushing Pig
Pig's stroller. It was full of Pig Pig and all the
groceries it took to feed him. Up the hill they
went. Slower and slower.

Pig Pig's mother puffed and grunted. She gave
the stroller just one more push and collapsed!

The stroller stopped at the top of the hill. It hung there and then, slowly, it moved over the top and started to roll down the other side. Faster and faster it went.

"Momma!" squealed Pig Pig.
"My baby!" gasped
Pig Pig's mother.
Pig Pig kept squealing as the
stroller careened down the hill.

Then horror filled
Pig Pig's eyes. Below him,
directly in his path,
was a baby carriage with
a *real* baby in it!

Pig Pig whirled into action. He stepped over the
front of the stroller and plunked both feet down
hard on the road.

In a cloud of dust, the stroller dragged to a stop
just inches from the sleeping baby.
Pig Pig had stopped the stroller and saved the baby!

The baby's mother kissed Pig Pig on the head.
"How can I ever thank you enough?" she cried.
"Such a brave young pig."

By the time Pig Pig's mother had run down the
hill, Pig Pig was surrounded by people. They
patted him on the back, and shook his hand, and
told him what a big brave pig he was.

Pig Pig beamed.

Pig Pig's mother hugged Pig Pig.

"I'm proud of you, my baby," she said. "You must be tired. Climb back into your stroller and let me push you home."

"No," said Pig Pig. "I'm not a baby anymore, and *you're* the one who must be tired. *You* get into the stroller, and I'll push *you* home."

And she did, and he did, and after that,
Pig Pig was never a baby again.

nickelodeon

RUSTY RIVETS

BOO GOES THERE?

BY **DAVID LEWMAN**
BASED ON THE TELEPLAY "RUSTY'S SPOOKY ADVENTURE" BY SCOTT GRAY

ILLUSTRATED BY
ARIANNA SABELLA, VALERIA ORLANDO AND **GIUSEPPE DI MAIO**
COLORING BY **TOMATO FARM**

A Random House PICTUREBACK® Book

Random House 🏠 New York

© 2018 Spin Master Ltd. All rights reserved. Published in the United States by Random House Children's Books, a division of Penguin Random House LLC, 1745 Broadway, New York, NY 10019, and in Canada by Penguin Random House Canada Limited, Toronto. Pictureback, Random House, and the Random House colophon are registered trademarks of Penguin Random House LLC. Rusty Rivets and all related titles, logos, and characters are trademarks of Spin Master Ltd. Nickelodeon, Nick Jr., and all related titles and logos are trademarks of Viacom International Inc.
rhcbooks.com
ISBN 978-1-5247-7275-8
MANUFACTURED IN CHINA
10 9 8 7 6 5 4 3 2 1

One moonlit night, Mr. Higgins told Rusty, Ruby, and Liam that he had planned the route for a *spoooooky* adventure walk around Sparkton Hills.

"Expect some fun surprises, and try not to get too scared!" he said.

Rusty and Liam cheered. "We love to be scared!" they said.

Ruby looked unsure.

"Your first stop is the ice cream shop!" said Mr. Higgins.

"How spooky is this adventure going to be?" Ruby asked nervously.

"Are you scared?" Rusty said.

"What? No!" she said, laughing. "I was just wondering how NOT scared I'm going to be!"

Liam and Rusty ran off to get ready.

Ruby decided to build something with Jack that would keep things from getting *too* spooky.

Ruby made the Ghost-Grabber 9000! She started with a jet-pack harness, added a spotlight to help her track ghosts, and then attached a net launcher to trap spooky things. "Modified. Customized. *Rubified!*" she said.

Rusty loved Ruby's new invention, but he had a question.
"You're sure you're not scared? If you are, we don't have to—"
"Nope!" Ruby insisted. "Not scared. Just prepared!"
She took a deep breath and followed Rusty, Jack, and Liam
to the ice cream shop.
"Welcome to the spookiest spot in town!" Sammy said.
"Some things are UP when they should be DOWN!"
He held up two ice cream scoops, then let go of them.

As Sammy headed out the door, the scoops—and other metal objects—floated to the ceiling!

"There has to be a perfectly good explanation for this," Ruby said.

"Yeah!" Liam agreed. "Like a GHOST!"

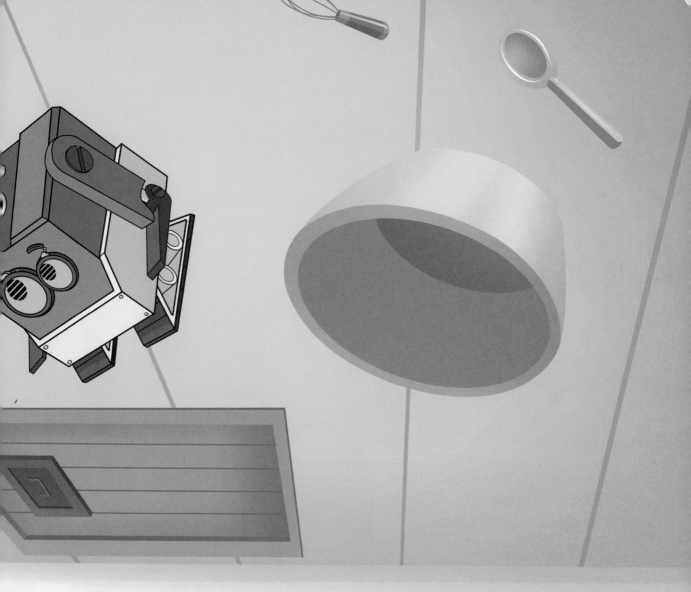

They heard a strange humming sound. Then Rusty's flashlight was yanked toward the ceiling!

"My flashlight!" he shouted.

"My MEEEEEE!" Ruby cried as she rose into the air, along with Jack!

"Look!" Rusty said. "Your Ghost-Grabber 9000 is lighting up a wire! I think there's something in the attic!"

Rusty was right. There was a giant electric magnet in the attic, pulling all the metal up to the ceiling!

"I'll turn it off," Rusty called. "Ready?"

Jack extended his foot to the floor to brace himself. Ruby held on to his arms.

Rusty flipped a switch. CRASH! All the metal objects fell to the floor! Jack safely lowered himself and Ruby.

Ruby was ready to go home. But their spooky adventure wasn't over yet. Sammy returned. "Ranger Anna could use your help with some ghostly monkey business over at the Animal Park," he said. "If you dare! BWA-HA-HA!"

"Welcome to the Animal Park," said Ranger Anna in a spooky voice, "where strange things happen after dark!" She pointed. Bananas were floating in the monkey cage!

"Maybe it's the magnet trick again?" Rusty said.

"But bananas aren't made of metal," Ruby said, staring at the floating fruit.

The bananas spun through the air, then flew right toward them!

The kids and Jack ducked behind some rocks.

"The monkeys' hands go right through the bananas!" he cried.

"That proves it! Those are GHOST bananas!" Liam said.

Ruby covered her face. Rusty said they could leave if she was too scared.

"I'm not scared!" she said. "I'm prepared! I've got my Ghost Grabber 9000!"

Ruby patted her machine, which accidentally launched a net.
It landed on . . . Mr. Higgins!

"You caught me!" he said, laughing. "Me and my banana
projector!" He switched the projector off. "Well, no more
spooky surprises until next year. Hope you had fun!"

Rusty, Ruby, Liam, and Jack hurried back to the Recycling Yard. They agreed that their night had been *spook*-tacular! Ruby claimed she hadn't been a bit scared.

Liam pointed behind them. "Look," he said. "A ghost!"

A little ghost floated in the air, giggling.

"AHHHH!" everyone screamed, and ran away. Jack hid under a box.

The ghost chased the kids all over the Recycling Yard. Just when they thought they'd lost it, it reappeared.

"BOO!" it said.

They ran into the Rivet Lab.

Ruby slumped to the floor. "Guys, I have a confession. I *am* scared."
"It's okay to admit you're scared," Rusty said, pulling her to her feet.
"AHHH!" Liam yelled, pointing. "GHOST!"
The giggling little ghost slowly flew over them.

Ruby decided she had to save her friends.
Even if she was scared, she was prepared.
She launched a net . . . but missed.
She gulped. "Oops!"
"What do we do now?" Liam cried.

Thinking quickly, Ruby asked Claw to toss her a robot arm. She attached the arm to her invention.

"All right, Ghost Grabber 9000," she said, opening and closing the hand on the robot arm. "Let's grab a ghost!"

Ruby chased the little ghost, trying to grab it with her new robot hand.
"This is awesome!" Rusty said to Liam. "Ruby's standing up to a ghost!"
After three tries, Ruby finally grabbed the ghost! But the "ghost" was really
just a small sheet, and underneath it was . . .

"WHIRLY?" Rusty and Liam exclaimed.

The little Bit giggled as Mr. Higgins stepped into the room.

"Ta-da! I hope you liked my spooky twist ending!" said Mr. Higgins.

"We sure did!" Rusty said.

"I was scared," Ruby said, "but it was awesome!"

Then a box moved across the floor all by itself!
"AHHHH!" everyone screamed.
Whirly lifted the box. Underneath it was . . . Jack!

"Thanks for a *spook*-tacular time, Mr. Higgins!" Rusty said.

"The best part was when Ruby stood up to the ghost for us!" said Liam.

"You guys would've done the same for me," said Ruby.

"Of course," Liam said. "But I'd rather stand up to a ghost for ICE CREAM!"

Everybody laughed. The night had been super spooky, but they had all LOVED it!